Me and My Pet CAT

Christine Morley and Carole Orbell

Illustrations by
Brita Granström

WORLD BOOK / TWO-CAN

First published in the United States by
World Book Inc.
525 W. Monroe
20th Floor
Chicago IL USA 60661
in association with Two-Can Publishing Ltd.

**For information on other World Book products,
call 1-800-255-1750, x 2238.**

ISBN: 0-7166-1750-1 (pbk.)
ISBN: 0-7166-1749-8 (hbk.)
LC: 96-60459

Printed in Hong Kong

1 2 3 4 5 6 7 8 9 10 99 98 97 96

Art Director: Carole Orbell
Senior Managing Editor: Christine Morley
Text: Nicole Carmichael
Additional design: Amanda McCourt and Helen Holmes
Consultant: Lisa Cobb, NCDL Animal Nurse of the Year 1995
Illustrator: Brita Granström
Photographer: Ray Moller
Thanks to: Tim Kelly, Jan and Katy Lambert

Contents

Perfect pets

Cats can make great pets. They can be easy to look after and very friendly, and you can have lots of fun playing with them. But good pets need good owners. So, to make sure you are the best, read on…

Furry and fierce!

Your pet cat may be cuddly and cute, but it has very wild relatives, such as the lion and the tiger! Its closest relative is the North African wildcat. The first pet cats were small wildcats that preferred being looked after by people to living in the wild.

Tiny tigers

In some ways, pet cats are similar to wild cats. They enjoy hunting, and they are also territorial. This means they try to keep other cats away from places that they think belong to them.

Tigers prowl and hunt on their own, just as pet cats do!

Super senses

Like most hunters, cats can see and hear very well—much better than humans. Your cat's twitchy nose is very good at sniffing out smells, and those whiskers help it to feel how close things are around it, especially in the dark.

Wild cats hunt for food, but pet cats hunt for fun.

5

Most cats are beautiful, playful, and cuddly—they make purrfect pets!

Rest and play

Cats have strong, bendy bodies that are great for sprinting, jumping, climbing, and balancing. But even though they're incredibly active, cats are also champion sleepers. They can doze for most of the day, almost anywhere!

All kinds of cats

Most cats are very similar in size and shape, but their coats can be all sorts of colors and patterns. They can also have long or short fur, and some breeds have almost no fur at all!

Furry facts
Did you know that the type of coat your cat has may be able to tell you something about its personality? Long-haired cats are supposed to be calm and quiet, while short-haired Oriental breeds, such as the Siamese, are thought to be excitable and noisy.

Most cats have soft, beautiful fur that keeps them warm.

I'm a pedigree, but some of my best friends are alley cats!

Amazing alley cats

A cat that is a mixture of different breeds is known as a crossbreed, or alley cat. Crossbreeds can be short or long haired, and their coats come in lots of different colors. They are not as expensive to buy as pedigreed cats, but they may be just as beautiful.

Time for a catnap before I start work!

Some cats aren't just pretty—they're useful, too. Farm cats earn their keep by catching mice.

Long-haired cats need to be brushed every day, so be prepared!

Aristocats!

Pedigreed cats are "purebred." This means that their parents, grandparents, and great-grandparents are the same breed. Pedigreed cats can be valuable and often win prizes at cat shows, but they may need more looking after than ordinary cats.

The right cat for you

Before you buy a cat, think about how much care it will need. As well as feeding and grooming it, you will need to give it lots of attention, especially if you buy a kitten.

Little and lovely

It's hard to resist fluffy kittens, but, like babies, they need lots of looking after. You'll have to teach them to use their own bathroom, called a litter box. It needs to be sifted clean every day. Kittens also need special food and lots of attention.

Make sure you can give your cats all the attention they need.

When is it my turn for a cuddle?

One of the family

You may want a new cat, but if you already have another pet, it might become jealous. Give your old pets lots of time to get used to the new arrival, and let them meet each other slowly. Don't leave them together to begin with because they may fight.

There are some pets your cat won't be friends with!

In or out?

If you don't have a yard, it won't be fair to get a cat that is used to going outside. Some cats are happy living indoors, and they avoid such dangers as cars or other animals.

Choosing your pal

You'll probably fall in love with every cat and kitten you see, but which one will you choose? Here are some things that you should look out for.

Do you want your cat to have kittens?

Hello there!
If you're buying a kitten, look for one that comes up to you as if it's saying hello. A lively kitten who's got its nose into everything will be much better at looking after itself.

Do you mind if your cat gets into fights?

Pick the nosy one—it'll be the most fun!

Boy or girl?
Boy cats, or tomcats, like to roam and often get into fights. They mark their territory by spraying a smelly liquid around. If you buy a girl cat, find out if she has had an operation to keep her from having kittens.

Shelter shopper

One of the best places to find a cat or a kitten is an animal shelter. They have lots of different types of cats and they can tell you about each cat's history and personality. If you want a pedigree, find someone who breeds them specially.

Nice and clean

Look closely at your new cat. Make sure that its eyes, ears, and nose are clean. Carefully open its mouth and check its teeth and gums. Then look at its coat, even underneath the tail, to make sure that it's not dirty.

Do you want to explore?

OK, but you go first!

Don't take a kitten home if it is less than six weeks old.

Are you ready?

Bringing your new cat home will be exciting for you, but a bit scary for your new pet—especially if it's just left its mother. Help it to settle in quickly by being properly prepared.

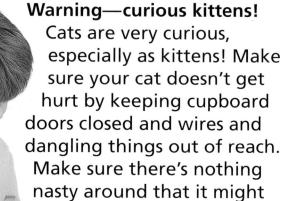

You won't need much to start off with, just food and water bowls, a collar, and a tag.

Make sure that your cat's collar is not too tight. You should be able to fit two fingers under it.

Home sweet home
Make your home as nice as you can for your new cat. Give it a bowl of tasty food, fresh water, and some toys to play with. Put a collar on it and give it lots of cuddles. Keep your pet indoors for at least two weeks, so it becomes used to its new home.

Warning—curious kittens!
Cats are very curious, especially as kittens! Make sure your cat doesn't get hurt by keeping cupboard doors closed and wires and dangling things out of reach. Make sure there's nothing nasty around that it might try to eat.

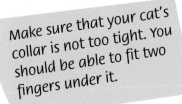
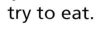

Catch the litterbug!

If your cat doesn't go outside, it'll need to use a litter box when it wants to go to the bathroom. Use a special scoop and rubber gloves to remove the dirty litter, and clean the whole box at least twice a week.

Keep an eye on your kitten—it may get into places it can't get out of!

It's a long way down...

Your cat may sleep in all kinds of strange places!

Sweet dreams

Put your cat's bed somewhere warm and quiet. A basket or a box lined with an old blanket will make a comfortable bed. But don't expect your pet just to sleep there. After a while, it'll catnap wherever it wants to!

Dinner time!

Whether you have a kitten or a grown-up cat, the right kind of food will help to keep your pet in tip-top cat condition.

What's on the menu?

When your cat is a kitten, you can feed it as many as four small meals every day. Your cat will stay healthy if you feed it a high-quality commercial cat food.

Now you know why I'm called Nibbles!

Grown-up cats need to be fed once a day, but some like to eat in the morning and the evening.

You can treat your cat to vegetables, cooked beef liver, or fish. But too many dairy products can make it sick.

What a treat!
Cats love a special treat from time to time. To keep your cat interested in its food, try changing brands regularly—this will prevent picky eating, too!

You can occasionally add bits of bread and vegetables to your cat's usual food, so it won't get bored.

Don't worry if your cat nibbles grass. It just likes the taste!

A mouse in the house
Your cat might grow up to be the best mouse catcher in town, but not because it's hungry. Hunting mice, birds, and insects is for fun, not for supper. When your cat presents you with a bird it has caught, it thinks it is giving you a present!

Favorite foods
The label on the can tells you how much food to give your cat. If your pet starts to get chubby, give it a bit less food and more exercise. Like you, there will be some foods that your cat likes a lot more than others. You'll soon learn what to put on the shopping list.

Ooops, it's been drinking milk again!

Neat and tidy

When it comes to keeping clean and tidy, cats have got it licked! They spend almost as long washing themselves as they do sleeping—which is good news for you!

After a bath, make sure you dry your cat quickly, so it doesn't catch a cold.

Brushing up

A short-haired cat should be combed twice a week, from its head down to the tip of its tail. A long-haired cat needs careful combing and brushing every day, because its fur can become very tangled.

Most cats love being groomed, as long as you do it very gently.

Bath time

If you have a long-haired cat that gets really dirty, you may have to give it a bath. Make sure the water is warm and not too deep. Use a special cat shampoo from a pet store, and wash the cat's head only if you really have to. When it's clean, wrap it in a towel and gently rub it dry.

Powder puss

Watch out for pesky pests called fleas. You can spot them in your cat's fur— they look like tiny, dark specks. You can buy special powder or a spray from the pet store to get rid of them.

But I like being dirty!

Don't shake on too much flea powder—just a little will do.

Most cats would rather play than have a bath!

Deep cleaning

You might need to use a damp cotton ball or a cotton swab to wipe your cat's eyes and ears (be careful not to push the swab far down in its ear). You also might need to brush its teeth. Your cat should have its own toothbrush and cat toothpaste—but baking soda will do just as well.

Keeping fit

You won't catch your cat running after sticks in the park, but your pet will still love to jump around and play different games, especially with you and your friends.

Strrrrretch!

Cats don't need as much exercise as you to keep them trim. Even cats that live indoors all the time keep fit just by doing big stretches and jumping on and off furniture. They also enjoy racing from room to room.

Kitten capers

Like babies, kittens sleep a lot. But when they're awake, it's playtime! They love to climb all over each other and explore everything. They also like to chase balls of string and toy mice and to pounce on squeaky toys.

Your cat has its own way of staying trim.

You don't need to take your cat out for walks. If you try, it'll probably take you!

Chasing a ball will keep you and your cat really fit.

Follow the leader

A few cats will let you take them out on a leash, but don't expect them to walk quietly next to you! You will have to follow them and be very careful not to pull them around. Make sure that they don't lead you up a tree!

I know—I'll hide behind this yellow thing.

Fun and games

When it comes to running, jumping, and playing, your cat will follow your lead. Try to play a few games with your pet every day. Otherwise, it might get bored and spend most of its day snoozing or meowing for attention.

Teaching time

No matter how smart your cat is, you won't be able to train it like a dog. But there are a few very important things that you should teach your pet.

House rules

If you have a new kitten, you must teach it to keep itself, and the house, clean. Even cats that go outside should know how to use a litter box.

Remember to clean the litter box regularly, or your kitten won't want to use it.

Show your pet the box, then hold its paws and gently scratch them in the litter. Do this a few times each day, until your cat starts using the box by itself.

Flap happy!

If your cat goes outdoors, the easiest way for it to get in and out of your home is through a cat flap. Show your pet how to push the flap with its paws. Then hold it open and tempt it through with a treat or a toy.

A cat flap with a clear window is best, so your cat can see what's on the other side.

Fish on a rope—my favorite toy!

Here, kitty kitty!

Say your cat's name whenever you give your pet food or play with it. This will help your cat to get used to your voice, so that it will come when you call it.

Some cats learn some really clever tricks all by themselves, such as how to open doors!

Naughty cat!

Kittens can be very naughty, but they don't know they're doing anything wrong. To correct your kitten, give it a gentle squirt of water from a plant sprayer. Your pet will quickly learn why it's being punished.

Yuk! I've got wet whiskers.

Catspeak

There are lots of ways a cat can tell you how it feels, from meowing and purring to the way it moves its body. Here are some clues to what your cat might be saying to you.

Hi there!
Your cat's way of saying hello is to meow loudly and rub its fur against you. Your pet might also lick your skin and push its claws into you. This is your cat's way of saying that it really likes you.

Most cats really enjoy being tickled behind their ears.

Cats like to rub against you so that they can leave their smell on you!

Purrfectly happy!
It's easy to spot a happy cat. It will be purring loudly, stretched out somewhere warm and comfortable, with its eyes half closed. Things that make cats happy are playing, being stroked and cuddled, and licking themselves clean, especially after a meal.

This is *my* yard!

"Go away" is something that cats say quite often. This is because they want to defend their territory from other cats. To scare them away, a cat will puff up its body to make itself look bigger. If a cat's very angry, it might hiss and spit.

Leave me alone

Once in a while, your cat might be annoyed or irritable. It will sit alone, flicking its tail from side to side. Your cat might hide somewhere dark and growl if you come near it.

This wall's not big enough for the both of us!

Oh dear, is there going to be trouble?

Checkups

As long as you look after your cat properly, it should stay healthy. Sometimes though, cats need special attention from you or your vet.

Always take your cat to the vet in a box or crate.

Vet visit

Soon after your cat has settled in at home, you should take it for a checkup at the vet's. The vet will check your pet all over and look inside its mouth and ears. She may listen to its heart with a special instrument, called a stethoscope.

That doesn't look like a bottle of milk.

The vet will be able to spot any problems, and she will make sure your cat has all its shots.

Fact finder

Every cat should have a pet-care card. You can make your own by writing down important information about your cat, such as how much it weighs and what shots it has had. Remember to take the card when you visit your vet.

Put your cat's photo on its pet-care card.

This won't hurt!

Your cat must have special shots, called vaccinations, to keep it from catching any cat diseases. Although your pet might be scared, the shots won't hurt much. Kittens can be vaccinated when they are nine weeks old.

Now I'm old enough to have my shots!

Remember— your cat will need booster shots every year.

Emergency!

Sometimes, it's easy to see when your cat is not feeling well. At other times, you may need to look for a few clues.

Food—no thanks!
Cats don't usually make a fuss when they're sick. Instead, they like to rest in a warm, quiet place. They will probably refuse to eat, and they definitely won't want to play. If your cat behaves like this, take it to the vet.

Kung-fu cats
Fighting is quite common for tomcats. If your cat comes home with bitten ears and a few scratches, give it a cuddle and ask the vet to look the cat over. Try to keep it indoors for a while, until it feels much better.

Sick cats like to be by themselves.

I don't feel well.

Aaaitchooo!
A cat can catch colds, just like you! You can keep your pet from getting colds, by taking it to the vet for a special shot. Do this as soon as you get your new cat.

A warm hot-water bottle tucked under a blanket will make a cosy bed for a sick cat.

Sick bay
If your cat is sick, make its bed as comfy as possible. Don't make a lot of noise around your pet, because it needs plenty of rest to get better.

I'm feeling better already!

Bits and pieces

There are lots of fun and useful things you can buy for your cat, from pretty collars to special toys. Why not add a few of these things to your cat's collection?

Cat collars

Your cat should always wear a collar and a tag. Some collars repel fleas, and others have a bell that you, and birds, can hear. Some collars are elastic, so your cat will not hurt itself if it gets caught on something.

Tons of toys

A cat needs lots of different toys to play with, especially if it is kept indoors all the time. Buy it furry mice to pounce on and chew and a light ball that it can bat with its paws and chase around the room.

Missed by a whisker!

Your local pet store will have lots of different toys and collars for you to choose from.

Happy traveler

The safest way to carry your cat is in a special box or crate. A cardboard box will work, but it won't last as long as a crate. Plastic crates have a carrying handle and a wire mesh door, so your cat can see where it's going.

Up to scratch

Most cats love to sharpen their claws, especially on the furniture! Train your cat to use a scratching post, which you can buy at a pet store. As soon as you see your cat clawing, carry it to the post. It'll soon get the hang of it.

I've got a good view from here.

Adventure playground

An activity center will give your cat plenty to do. You can buy one or ask an adult to make one. It could have a scratching post in the middle and a box at the top for your cat to hide in. Hang some toys from the top and watch your cat try to catch them.

Sprinkle catnip, an herb that cats love, on an activity center, and they'll play for hours!

Amazing cats

Cats are amazing creatures! They can climb great heights, run fast and are deadly hunters. In fact, they are so special, they were treated as gods in ancient Egypt!

Clever claws
A cat called Towser caught a record-breaking number of mice. She lived in a factory and caught a total of 28,899 mice in her life.

Dusty was a tabby cat who lived in Texas. During her life, she gave birth to 420 kittens!

Cats have great balance!

High life!
In 1950, a kitten followed some climbers up the Matterhorn mountain in Switzerland, which is 4,897 yards high.

Pampered pets

The ancient Egyptians loved cats. They treated them as gods and made offerings to their statues. If someone was found to have killed a cat, that person would be sentenced to death!

Catspeak

Did you know that a lion's roar can be heard up to 3 miles away? Although big cats can roar, they cannot purr. Your pet cat is a great purrer, but it can't roar.

All cat's whiskers have their own pattern, just like fingerprints on people. No two sets are the same.

Useful words

booster These are shots that your cat needs to have every year to protect it against diseases.

breed A special type of cat, such as a Siamese or a chinchilla.

crossbreed or alley cat A cat whose parents are different breeds.

feline Another word for a cat or something that is like a cat.

furball When a cat licks itself clean, it swallows some of its hair. These hairs make a ball in its stomach, and it will sometimes cough these up.

kennel This is a place where you can leave your cat when you go on a vacation. The staff there will feed and care for your pet until you come back.

neutering An operation that male and female cats have to keep them from breeding, or having kittens.

pedigree Cats whose parents, grandparents and great-grandparents are all the same breed. They often have a special certificate to prove this.

queen The name for a female cat that has not been neutered.

spraying This is something that a male cat does to mark his territory and keep other cats away.

tomcat The name of a male cat that has not been neutered. Tomcats spend lots of time, especially at night, walking around their territory and defending it from other cats.

vaccinations These are shots that cats get to keep them from catching diseases from other cats. After your cat is vaccinated, it will need to have yearly booster shots as well.